PRAYING WITH CONFIDENCE
Overcoming Disappointment In Prayer

CONTENTS

The Trouble
With Prayer 2

Returning To
The Basics

Approach God
Through A Mediator 6

Be Honest About
Your Complaints 9

Converse
Instead Of Talk 18

Defer To
God's Perspective 22

Enjoy God
While You Wait 26

Praying Through
The Bible 29

Your Next Prayer 32

Disappointment has a way of turning prayers into silence. It can be hard to pray when you are bitter and angry toward people you believe are ruining your life. It can be even harder to pray when you feel that God Himself has let you down.

God understands our feelings. Yet He has made a way for us to come with confidence to His throne of grace. In the following pages, David Egner offers help to those who have lost confidence in God and in their own ability to know that He is listening when they pray.

Martin R. De Haan II

Managing Editor: David Sper
Cover Photo: TSW/Ed Simpson
Scripture quotations are from the New King James Version. Copyright © 1982 by Thomas Nelson, Inc. Used by permission. All rights reserved.
© 1993, 2002 RBC Ministries, Grand Rapids, Michigan
Printed in USA

THE TROUBLE WITH PRAYER

In front of me sat a group of adult singles who were gathered to do a study on prayer. I handed out a sheet of paper that began with this statement: "When it comes to prayer, I _____." They were to fill in the blank.

How would you respond? Before we go on, it might be helpful for you to do just that. Complete this sentence:

When it comes to prayer, I _____.

When I tabulated what the group had written, the results fell into these categories:
- "I don't pray enough."
- "I don't know what to pray."
- "I don't know if prayer does any good."

I've found such answers common. While a few speak glowingly of the ease with which they slip in and out of conversations with God, more seem to view prayer as a struggle that is sometimes won but more often lost.

It is understandable that prayer would not always come easily. Rightly understood, it is not just emotion addressed to God. It is also an expression of faith that is often weak and small. It is a weapon of spiritual warfare that is used to fight for contested ground. It is a reflection of a relationship with God that is often disrupted and strained by our own ignorance, inattention, and insensitivity. It is an expression of confidence in God that is often replaced by feelings of disappointment.

Early in our Christian walk, we pray with high expectations. We assume that God will give us the deepest desires of our heart, and that through prayer we will experience the closeness and happiness we long for. With our confidence in God we believe that we will rise above any problem.

Then we ask God for something important to us and we don't get it. We assure ailing friends that we are praying for their recovery, but they don't get better. We pray in the presence of our family for a solution to problems that are affecting them, only to be left waiting for months and months while God seems to ignore us. We plead earnestly and often for our loved ones' spiritual restoration, but they remain cold toward God.

Slowly, disappointment forms. We lose our enthusiasm for prayer. Soon we're praying only at mealtimes. We go through a phase when we won't bring anything we really care about to the Lord because we can't take another rejection. We stop communicating with God.

Think a minute about your prayer relationship with God. If you've stopped growing in prayer, is it because of honest disappointment?

- **Disappointment With God.** "I asked and believed that God was going to heal my daughter. But she lost her fight with cancer anyway. I'm brokenhearted and confused."

- **Disappointment With Others.** "I have a hard time praying when I am so angry with people who are ruining my life."

- **Disappointment With Ourselves.** "I've wanted to pray. I've looked forward to it. I've had the best of intentions. But I just haven't been able to get around to it."

It takes faith and courage to work through a disrupted human relationship. It's the same in our relationship with God. The first step is to admit the problem. Then we must work past the disappointment and regain our confidence in God. The remainder of this booklet is written to help build that confidence.

But before we go on, let me speak personally for a moment. I know a little of what it means to be disappointed with the turns and twists of life. Sometimes the most disturbing experiences have involved what God has allowed in the lives of those closest to my heart. One of those times involved the health of a dear grandson. Nathan was born with an immune deficiency. His tiny body had no mechanism for fighting disease. In the first few years of his life, we watched helplessly as little Nathan struggled through a series of upper respiratory infections. God didn't seem to be answering our pleas. Hospitalizations were common.

As a family we were frightened. Could we trust God even if He didn't answer our prayers for this one so dear to our hearts?

Doctors told us that the immune system in 60 percent of these children "kicks in" about the time they turn 3. While that information offered some hope, it also left us with the realization that 40 percent do not develop defenses against infection. Time after time, I looked at that defenseless little body and prayed.

At first I was consumed by the "what ifs" of Nathan's condition. As time went on, the focus of my prayers changed. I was no longer as absorbed in the pain I was feeling. I found myself using fewer words. I wrestled, often in silence, on Nathan's behalf. Eventually I was saying simply, "God, do what's best. Only You know, and I trust You and Your goodness. I want so much for You to heal him. Yet, Your will be done."

"When I am in the presence of God, it seems profoundly unbecoming to demand anything."
Francis Schaeffer

About the time Nate turned 3, he began to have fewer infections. Then new tests came back: God mercifully let Nathan be one of the 60 percent who overcome immune deficiency.

Through such uncontrollable circumstances of life I have been learning to trust God in the school of prayer. Sometimes I have been grateful for His "yes." Sometimes I've seen the wisdom of a "no." Sometimes I've even learned to enjoy God in the process of waiting for His answer.

Yet I still find myself lapsing into the discouragement of circumstances. I find myself longing for the kind of power that would give me Elijah-like control over physical conditions (Jas. 5:16-18). What I've learned in time, however, is that real confidence in prayer isn't found by projecting my desires upon God. Instead, I have found confidence by learning some simple yet profound principles of prayer. They do not depend on our ability to be eloquent or spiritually insightful. They have ABC-like qualities that are learned in our Lord's school of prayer.

RETURNING TO THE BASICS

APPROACH GOD THROUGH A MEDIATOR

Mediation was God's idea. He knew we had a problem trusting Him. But He could not ignore what we were doing. So God offered mediation. To resolve the differences that had come between us, He sent One who could understand and be sympathetic to our condition while at the same time representing the interests of heaven.

This Mediator so identified with us and became so involved in our problems that He ended up crying out, "My God, My God, why have You forsaken Me?" (Mk. 15:34). Yet, 3 days after that inexpressible moment, it became clear that the Mediator had been victorious. Through His great sacrifice, our Mediator had removed the barrier that had disrupted our relationship with God.

We would still sin. We would still be blinded by our own desires and stubborn pride. We would still find ourselves filled with regret. We would still become confused about what God was doing in our lives. But never again would we have reason to doubt the Father's love for us. Never again could it be persuasively argued that the Father didn't care, that He wasn't touched by our problems, or that He had left us to die in our circumstances. Never again would we have to approach

God in prayer without the assurance that He wanted to talk with us far more than we wanted to talk to Him.

Without this mediatorial work, we might have wondered if God would even listen to us when we prayed. We might assume from our circumstances that He didn't care. But now memory of what happened on the Mediator's cross can restore confidence in us whenever we approach God in prayer. Now we can take courage in the fact that we don't have to approach God in our own sin-stained reputation. We don't come to Him in our own name. We don't approach Him with our own carefully chosen words. We come to Him in the merits of the One who paid for all of our sins with His own blood. We come to God in the name and interests of His own and dearly loved Son, Jesus Christ.

Confidence In A Past Sacrifice. This manner of approach has always been in God's mind for us. Long before our Mediator's arrival, the design for such an approach to God was illustrated in the tabernacle and temple worship of Israel. For many centuries God had made it clear that His people must approach Him on the basis of a blood sacrifice. But only in the coming and suffering of Christ do we see that those sacrifices illustrated the violent suffering and death of God's own Son.

There was in the same temple, in a place that signified the very Presence of God, an altar of incense. This burning incense, by its fragrance and ascending motion, symbolized prayers that please God. Significantly, this incense was lit by a coal from the altar of sacrifice (Ex. 30:7-

10). In God's mind, there is a connection between the sacrifice and the prayers by which we approach Him.

This link between sacrifice and prayer is what our Mediator secured for us. He offered a sacrifice acceptable to God. Then He encouraged us to go into the presence of God in His own name. Of this basis for confidence, the author of Hebrews wrote:

> *Seeing then that we have a great High Priest who has passed through the heavens, Jesus the Son of God, let us hold fast our confession. For we do not have a High Priest who cannot sympathize with our weaknesses, but was in all points tempted as we are, yet without sin. Let us therefore come boldly to the throne of grace, that we may obtain mercy and find grace to help in time of need (Heb. 4:14-16).*

Being in the presence of God is described in this passage as like being in a throne room. In Europe and the Middle East, the throne rooms of kings were ornately and elaborately decorated and filled with attendants. Common people felt inferior and intimidated—the very feelings we might have as we approach God in prayer. But through the mediation and understanding of Christ, we can walk confidently into the presence of God without feeling like an unwanted intruder. We come in the name and merits of the Son of God, and that gives us access to the Father at any time. We have an invitation stamped with the royal seal to pray at any time, under any conditions, whatever our circumstances or needs, because this is a "throne of grace." Grace is undeserved kindness. Grace is unmerited assistance. This is the kind of help our Mediator has secured for us.

Confidence In A Present Advocate.

There's more! We can come to "the throne of grace" with confidence in our Mediator because His work for us continues. Even now He is at the right hand of God interceding on our behalf (Rom. 8:34). On the merit of His sacrifice, the Lord Jesus is our Intercessor. He is with the Father in the throne room, speaking on our behalf. The apostle John expressed it this way:

> *If anyone sins, we have an Advocate with the Father, Jesus Christ the righteous. And He Himself is the propitiation [the atoning sacrifice] for our sins (1 Jn. 2:1-2).*

Why do we hold back? How could we feel hesitant or unworthy to pray when Jesus Christ Himself, on the basis of His sacrifice, is right now with the Father interceding for us?

BE HONEST ABOUT YOUR COMPLAINTS

God loves honest talk. Realism is at the heart of His own character. He hates darkness and deception. Darkness is the domain of His enemy. Therefore, a second essential to confidence in prayer is to learn to be honest about what is in our hearts. He can handle our complaints, our foolishness, our fears, and our failures. He won't be surprised or threatened by our anger, our confusion, or our childlike pleadings.

What does not please God are the cheap lies of flattery, ritual praise, insincere words repeated over and over without regret for what is really happening in our own soul. We need to put away our practices of fearful coverup, our sophisticated deceit, and our formal language, and instead lay the foundation of truth as the basis for prayer.

Prayers filled with pious lies are unacceptable to God, and they do not reflect the true spirit of our own hearts. That is why, in order to enter the throne room of grace and begin to pray with confidence, we must learn to be truthful when we pray. To do this, we have to spend time in self-evaluation and confession of sin. We must tell God how we really feel about Him, about ourselves, about our problems with people, and about our needs, frustrations, desires, and painful memories. We must also be honest about our desire to know His will and make it our own. If we don't want to do His will, then that too must be brought to the light so that we can ask God to help us overcome our rebellion and foolishness.

Confidence In God's Ability To Help Us Understand Ourselves. When we want to know the truth about ourselves, the Lord who knows our hearts will help us to see what is happening in us. The psalmist wrote, "O Lord, You have searched me and known me" (Ps. 139:1). David said to Solomon, "The Lord searches all hearts and understands all the intent of the thoughts" (1 Chr. 28:9).

The prayer of self-examination, when combined with the Scriptures, enables us to see what's really going on inside. The Bible shows us our deep-seated feelings and true motives. It takes us into the nooks and crannies where we hide old grudges and secret hatreds and bitter resentments. Through honest prayer we can bring these things to the surface, see them for what they really are, and ask God to help us deal with them.

We need to put away our formal language of prayer and lay the foundation of truth.

Of this we can be confident: If we ask God to show us our hearts, He will do it. Perhaps not immediately. But over time and in His own way, the Lord will pull back the curtains of denial and repression and show us ourselves. And He will take good care of us while He's doing it.

- He might bring an old hurt to mind for us to deal with and forget.
- He might remind us of a promise we have not kept or a debt we have not paid.
- He might let us feel the hurt we gave to someone else, perhaps many years ago, and tell us to make it right.
- He might direct us to straighten out a misunderstanding or forgive someone.

Heart knowledge is a wonderful, liberating gift, and it comes through being honest with the Lord in prayer.

Self-examination can also reveal the positive blessings in our lives. God is working in us and doing things for us all the time. He shows us His goodness, fills us with grace, helps us grow through adversity, sustains us through difficult circumstances, gives us ways to escape temptation, and grants us His peace. But when we're caught up in the details of life and distracted by responsibilities, we are sometimes oblivious to these things.

Confidence In God's Willingness To Forgive An Honest Heart.
It was the bottom of the 9th inning and the score was tied. The opposing team had the bases loaded with two outs. A hard grounder was hit a little to the right of the rookie shortstop. It bounced off his glove. The run scored and the game was lost. He had made that play a thousand times before—but not that time.

That ballplayer could have done what a lot of us do. He could have claimed that the ball hit a rock and took a bad bounce. He could have blamed the sun or the wet grass. But he didn't. "I blew it," he said after the game. "I take responsibility. It was my fault."

We need that attitude toward God. When the Lord convicts us of sin, we need to admit it, confess it, and then believe in God's willingness to forgive us.

Remember the story of David and Nathan? Corrupted by power, David turned the war over to his generals and stayed at home. He looked lustfully at a bathing Bathsheba, had her brought to the palace, committed adultery, then had her husband killed to cover up his sin. It appeared that he would get away with it—until he was confronted by Nathan the prophet with those undeniable words of condemnation, "You are the man!" (2 Sam. 12:7).

Finally, after days and probably many months of living in self-imposed darkness, David acknowledged his sin. His moving prayer of repentance is recorded in Psalm 51. "I acknowledge my transgressions," he confessed to the Lord, "and my sin is always before me. Against You, You only, have I sinned" (vv.3-4). David pleaded for a restoration to the joy he once had, and his prayer was answered by the forgiveness of God. The Bible, the Holy Spirit, and God's people serve as our Nathans today.

We live in a calloused world of hardened hearts and desensitized consciences. Lawyers can argue cases with skill and apparent sincerity even when they know the defendant is guilty. Sentences for horrible crimes are received without a sign of guilt or remorse. We are experts at denial and rationalization and finding someone else to blame.

How can we soften our hearts? We're so accustomed to an iron-shelled coldness. How do we get "a broken and a contrite heart" (Ps. 51:17) that is always accepted by the Lord? Ask for it. "Create in me a clean heart," we must plead. "Renew a steadfast spirit within me" (v.10). God will honor that prayer. He doesn't turn away when we pray, "God, be merciful to me a sinner!" (Lk. 18:13).

To be immediately right, say from your heart the truth about your wrongs.

Confidence In God's Ability To Handle Our Complaints. Our human relationships are cluttered with disagreements, struggles, and conflict. If there are none, someone is just suppressing it and postponing a confrontation until the future. Friends and lovers talk about their negative feelings openly and work through their differences. That should also be true in our relationship with God. We are free to respectfully and reverently disagree, question, and even argue with Him in prayer.

Rabbi Joseph Telushkin writes of the need for honest confrontations with God as being a legacy of the Jewish people. In his book *Jewish Literacy* he writes:

> [The] first instance of a human being arguing with God becomes a characteristic feature of the Hebrew Bible, and of Judaism in general. Hundreds of years after Abraham, the psalmist called out to God in anger and anguish: "Awake! Why do You sleep, O Lord? . . . Why do You hide Your face, and forget our affliction and our oppression?" (Ps. 44:23-24; see Habakkuk 1:2 and the entire book of Job for other examples of prophets or righteous men questioning God's ways). The willingness to confront the Almighty stems from the belief that God, like man, has responsibilities, and deserves criticism when He fails to fulfill them. Elie Wiesel, a Jew who stands in this tradition, has declared: "The Jew may love God, or he may fight with God, but he may not ignore God."

This seems to have been Abraham's attitude. God was about to destroy the wicked city of Sodom. Abraham interceded with the Lord, asking that the city be spared if 50 righteous people could be found. They could not. So, step by step, Abraham pleaded with God to reduce the number to 10. But when 10 could not be found, Sodom was destroyed (Gen. 18:23-33).

Moses also disagreed with God. The Lord had

performed miracle after miracle to deliver Israel from Egyptian bondage and provide for them in the wilderness. But while Moses was in the heights of Mount Sinai receiving the Law from the hand of the Lord, his countrymen were getting ready to give up on the One who had delivered them from Egypt. In violation of the first commandments God had given Moses, they made an idol of gold and used it as an excuse to indulge in the sexual abandon of pagan fertility worship. "Now therefore, let Me alone," God said to Moses, "that My wrath may burn hot against them and I may consume them" (Ex. 32:10). God even said He would start over again and make a great nation out of Moses.

Moses didn't want to give in. He pleaded with the Lord to spare Israel, "Why should the Egyptians speak, and say, 'He brought them out to harm them, to kill them in the mountains, and to consume them from the face of the earth'? Turn from Your fierce wrath, and relent from this harm to Your people" (v.12). God relented, and the Jews were spared (v.14).

Abraham and Moses are good examples for us. We too can clear the air with God. While still fearing God, and remembering to reverence Him, we can:

- Ask Him why He's waiting so long to save our loved one.
- Express our anger and disappointment because our child was not spared.
- Pour out our frustration to Him because we haven't found a job yet.
- Cry out to Him because we are still childless.

Such complaints do not threaten God. He knows we will never find a moral weakness in Him. He encourages us to be honest with Him so that we can discover the thoughts and feelings that are in our hearts. Once we bring them to the light, we can ask God to help us deal with them.

> *"The point of prayer is not to get answers from God; the goal of prayer is perfect and complete oneness with God."*
> Oswald Chambers

Why are we so hesitant to be honest with God? Perhaps we're the kind of people who avoid all conflict. We won't even tell our loved ones or friends any of our negative feelings. Or we may think it would be a lack of faith to challenge God.

Many of us have accepted society's idea that struggle and love do not go together. We assume that a relationship is good only as long as there is peace and harmony. The fact remains that we struggle in relationships because we really do care. And finding the courage to struggle and take risks and confront is what strengthens and deepens all relationships. The same is true in our relationship with God. Like Jacob at Bethel, we do well to wrestle with God once in a while. It can bring us His blessing (Gen. 32:24-32).

Confidence In What God Wants For Us. The goal of the believer in Jesus Christ is to become one (in heart and agreement) with God. When we come to Him in prayer, we need to be honest with ourselves about whether our desires are His desires, whether our will is His will, whether our requests would be His requests.

How do we grow in this "oneness" with God? Certainly we can never share in His complete understanding of all things. Yet, as we pray for the daily needs of life, for our spouse and children and friends, for healing or employment or guidance, we can do so with the same attitude of heart Jesus had in mind when He taught His disciples to pray to the Father, "Your will be done on earth as it is in heaven" (Mt. 6:10).

Jesus Himself expressed that same attitude a few hours before His death. He concluded an agonizing prayer session in Gethsemane—a time when He even asked the Father to let Him avoid the cross—with these words: "Nevertheless not My will, but Yours, be done" (Lk. 22:42). This surrender, after an intense, honest struggle, kept Him in a spirit of oneness with His Father.

We may have questions about praying, "Your will be done." Does that mean we are secretly giving up on what we just prayed for? Are we not saying that our prayer was offered without the true conviction that it was right and that God should answer it? Are we not falsely humble in trying not to bother God with our little wishes, and saying, "That's okay. I understand," if He does not grant our requests? If so, we've got it all wrong!

Helmut Thielicke wrote: This is just what the words "Thy will be done" do *not* mean. They mean, "Thou understandest my prayer better than I understand it myself (Rom. 8:26). Thou knowest most whether I need hunger or bread. Whatever may come, I will still say, 'Yes, dear

Lord' (Mt. 15:27). For I know that in everything, no matter what it may be, Thy will gives me fulfillment—beyond my asking and my comprehension."

When we pray "Your will be done," we are choosing to agree with God. We are saying to Him what Jesus said to His disciples, "My food is to do the will of Him who sent Me" (Jn. 4:34). And we are echoing the Lord's prayer in Gethsemane. Whether or not He gives us bread or a job or a mate or a child, His will done His way is best.

We will not discover the confidence of being in agreement with God, however, if we have not first been honest about the thoughts and emotions of our own hearts. Integrity of soul is basic to overcoming disappointment with God and developing confidence in prayer.

CONVERSE INSTEAD OF TALK

A common hindrance to confident praying is the feeling that no one is listening. We feel like the wife who tries to talk to her husband while he is reading the sports page of the newspaper or the father who is talking to his teenagers while they are listening to music. No feedback, no response, not even an occasional, "Uh-huh."

When this happens, we begin to see prayer as nothing more than ritual. We have lost sight of the truth that God is deeply interested in us and listening intently to every word of our prayers.

Prayer is intended to be a spirited interaction between us and a loving Being with whom we have an intimate and growing relationship. "We have almost forgotten," wrote A. W. Tozer in *Pursuit Of God,* "that God is a person and, as such, can be cultivated [in a relationship] as any person can." When we feel that God is not listening, we need to focus on two vital aspects of prayer.

Confidence In Listening To God. Prayer is not merely what we say to God. It is responding thoughtfully to what He has already said and what He is constantly saying to us through His Word. For this reason, the Bible is an important part of our ongoing conversation with the Lord.

One way to develop conversation with God is to open the Scriptures to a psalm or paragraph from one of the Epistles. Read thoughtfully to discover what the text is telling you about the thoughts, affections, and values of God. Listen carefully and reverently to the mind of the One who inspired these words. Ask Him to help you discover the interests and desires of His heart. Then respond conversationally from your own heart to what you are hearing. As you do, you will begin to develop confidence that you know what is important to God. You will also begin to discover what God is doing in your own heart.

As a husband prays in response to the words of 1 Corinthians 13, for example, he will know God's mind about love and apply it to his relationship with his wife. It may be the words *love is patient* that impress him about how tersely he's been treating her. This, in turn, should lead to a welcome and much-needed change in his attitude and behavior.

"Be silent," Francois Fénelon wrote, "and listen to God. Let your heart be in such a state of preparation that His Spirit may impress upon you such virtues as will please Him. This silence of all outward and earthly affection and of human thoughts within us is essential if we are to hear this voice."

It won't be an audible voice. But you will know it's the voice of the Spirit when you hear the truths of Scripture speaking gently, lovingly, and forcefully to the circumstances and concerns of your life.

One night when my grandson Nathan was extremely ill, I awakened and prayed for him. While I remained in an attitude of prayer, silent before the Lord, I became aware of a way I had not been sensitive to the needs of my wife, Shirley. I saw how my attitudes had not been in line with the words and heart of God. I recognized a need in her life that I had been blind to for years. I asked God's forgiveness and help. The next day I began to make the appropriate change in behavior toward her. What a difference it has made! I am convinced that is how God may speak to us when we are silent before Him.

Confidence In Responding To God. Listening to God will lead to actions as well as words. Words are just the beginning. If we're reading 1 Corinthians 15, for example, we will exalt the Lord for the great victory of the resurrection and the hope that goes with it. But our response will go beyond that. It will give us greater confidence as we face a defeated spiritual enemy. It will give us words to say to the terminally ill. It will give us power as we face the everyday tumults of life. It may cause us to forsake a sinful attitude or habit.

> *"Do not use the excuse of prayer to cover up what you know you ought to do."*
> Oswald Chambers

When we pray, we must be ready to take action. The deeper the prayer goes into the Scripture, into the mind of God, the more radical the action may be. It may lead us to someone's living room to share a deep burden. It may carry us back into the past to deal with some unresolved hurt we have received or inflicted. It may drastically change our plans. We may end up in some strange place doing things we never thought we would or could do. This is because our prayer is to God, and He is not a placid, inert Being. He is the living God, who steps into our lives with His awesome power and changes us in dramatic and unpredictable ways as we respond to Him. Or He may leave us right where we are. That's okay. He's God!

When we bow before God with our needs and our requests, we think we're the initiators. But it may be that all prayer is a response to Him. This is what Norway's Ole Hallesby taught in his classic book, *Prayer*. He saw Jesus' words "Behold, I stand at the door and knock" (Rev. 3:20) as the key that opens the door to prayer. And how does Christ knock? Through the conditions and circumstances of our experience that drive us to Him in prayer. As I think of it, my prayers for little Nathan were a response. Jesus had been knocking on the door of my life through the physical needs of my grandson.

DEFER TO GOD'S PERSPECTIVE

You've had it happen to you, I'm sure. You call the auto dealer and ask for the service department. "Can you hold?" the cheerful voice says. In a few seconds the "elevator music" starts. Every so often a recording assures you that your call will be answered. You wait and wait, imagining that an inane conversation about last night's ball game or some television program is keeping you in limbo. After a while you're ready to hang up. It would take less time to get in the car and drive over to the place!

Sometimes it seems that God has put us on hold. He may be doing some great things in our lives, but our deepest, most cherished request is not being granted. We know He's still there, but He is simply not responding.

Hannah of the Old Testament knew what it was like to feel rejected by God (1 Sam. 1:1-18). She was one of two women married to a man named Elkanah. Peninnah, the other wife, had borne him children, but Hannah was barren in a day when childlessness was considered a sign of God's displeasure. To make matters worse, Peninnah took cruel delight in mocking Hannah's barrenness whenever the family made their annual trip to the house of God to offer a sacrifice.

Hannah's distress lasted for years even though she

was a devout and faithful woman. She prayed and prayed. Yet God didn't answer. On one trip to the house of God "she was in bitterness of soul, and prayed to the Lord and wept in anguish" (v.10).

But that is not the end of Hannah's story. In God's time, and at just the right time, God gave Hannah a son. She became the mother of Samuel (vv.19-20), who in time would become a priest and prophet who would change the course of history.

In God's time, Hannah's sense of spiritual rejection was changed to joy. In an overwhelming song of praise to God, Hannah showed that her deepest longing was not for a son but to know that she was accepted and approved by God (2:1-10). In time, Hannah's bitterness was turned to joy. For every generation to come, her experience would show that what counts is not whether God immediately answers our prayers. The issue is whether we are humbly waiting on His wisdom and timing.

When Hannah's experience is combined with the rest of Scripture, we begin to see some of the many reasons for deferring not to our emotions but to the wisdom of God.

Confidence In God's Perspective. Our perspective is like looking through a pinhole. We can't see the whole picture. If we could, we would see that what we long for may not be good for us or for those we love. How many times I have been thankful that God has not given me everything I've asked Him for. How much better off I would have been if I had tempered my prayers with the awareness that it is only when we get to heaven that we will see the whole picture. Then we "shall know just as [we] also

[are] known" (1 Cor. 13:12). P. T. Forsythe wrote, "We shall come one day to a heaven when we shall gratefully see that God's great refusals were sometimes the truest answers to our prayers."

Confidence In God's Wisdom. God knows our deepest need. A single mother prayed for $2,000 to bring her financial relief. God denied the request as she expressed it. Instead of giving her the money, God gave her a job that she could handle. Then He gave her a friend who helped her to learn to manage her finances. In time she was able to look back and see that God did answer her request, but in a way that reflected His wisdom. The best part is that she grew in her trust in God.

Confidence In God's Timing. The house sells later than we wanted or the baby arrives 2 weeks sooner than we expected. God's timing is always best because of His ability to orchestrate the circumstances of our lives.

"One day . . . we shall gratefully see that God's great refusals were sometimes the truest answers to our prayers."
P. T. Forsythe

Confidence In God's Goodness. We may have prayed a long time for our wife or husband to treat us with more respect, but that does not happen until God leads us to stop downgrading our spouse in public.

The answer may not come because we are refusing to forgive someone, or we are controlled by an obsession, or we are seething in such anger that our holiness is corrupted. Or we "ask amiss" so that we can indulge some base desire (Jas. 4:3). We need to do the work of examination, confession, and repentance before our prayer is answered.

Oswald Chambers understood that waiting is part of prayer. About the verse, "Men always ought to pray and not lose heart" (Lk. 18:1), he wrote:

> Jesus taught His disciples the prayer of patience. If you are right with God and God delays the answer to your prayer, don't misjudge Him. Don't think of Him as an unkind friend, or an unnatural father, or an unjust judge, but keep at it. Your prayer will certainly be answered, for "everyone who asks receives." Pray and do not cave in. Your heavenly Father will explain it all one day. He cannot just yet because He is developing your character. "Forget the character," you say. "I want Him to grant my request." And He says, "What I am doing far exceeds what you can see or know. Trust Me."

The psalmist Asaph learned to overcome such disillusionment when he was reminded of the wider perspective of God. In Psalm 73 he said:

> *Truly God is good to Israel, to such as are pure in heart. But as for me, my feet had almost stumbled; my steps had nearly slipped. For I was envious of the boastful, when I saw the prosperity of the wicked. For there are no pangs in their death, but their strength is firm. They are not in trouble as other men . . . . Surely I have cleansed my heart in vain, and washed my hands in*

innocence. For all day long I have been plagued, and chastened every morning. If I had said, "I will speak thus," behold, I would have been untrue to the generation of Your children. When I thought how to understand this, it was too painful for me—until I went into the sanctuary of God; then I understood their end. Surely You set them in slippery places; You cast them down to destruction. Oh, how they are brought to desolation, as in a moment! They are utterly consumed with terrors. As a dream when one awakes, so, Lord, when You awake, You shall despise their image. Thus my heart was grieved, and I was vexed in my mind. I was so foolish and ignorant; I was like a beast before You. Nevertheless I am continually with You; You hold me by my right hand. You will guide me with Your counsel, and afterward receive me to glory. Whom have I in heaven but You? And there is none upon earth that I desire besides You. My flesh and my heart fail; but God is the strength of my heart and my portion forever (Ps. 73:1-5,13-26).

ENJOY GOD WHILE YOU WAIT

The psalmist Asaph showed us that there is more to trusting God than deferring to His wisdom. Another way to become confident in prayer is to learn to actually enjoy Him while waiting for Him to meet your needs.

Nothing we are waiting for can begin to compare with the privilege of knowing Him. Nothing else is as important to us as God Himself.

Certainly there are times when we will be overwhelmed by our troubles and crushed by our sense of disappointment and grief. Like Hannah, we will have times when we are beside ourselves with frustrated longings. Yet there will also be many other times when we can laugh for joy because of what God is doing for us.

Confidence In What You Know About Him.

As we learn to wait for God, we can begin to find delight in what we already know about Him. We can accept the invitation of the psalmist to enter His gates with thanksgiving and His courts with praise, and to bless His name (Ps. 100:4).

Thank Him. God has done so much for you. If your boss or parents had done one-tenth that much for you, you would express your gratitude in lavish terms. Do the same with God.

O Lord my God, I will give thanks to You forever (Ps. 30:12).

Jesus gave thanks to the Father (Lk. 10:21). Paul's prayers were filled with expressions of gratitude (Eph. 5:20). We too should give joyful thanks to the Lord.

Praise Him. We praise God for who He is and we thank Him for what He has done. The Bible is brimming with expressions of praise to the Lord.

Praise, O servants of the Lord, praise the name of the Lord! Blessed be the name of the Lord from this time forth and forevermore! From the rising of the sun to its going down the Lord's name is to be praised (Ps. 113:1-3).

Other passages of praise to the Lord include Psalm 146:1-2, Hebrews 13:15, and Revelation 4:11. Lift your praise up to God in your prayer. Express your worship and adoration in praise. "He is your praise" (Dt. 10:21).

Confidence In What He Has Promised.

Another way to enjoy God is to rejoice in the promises He gives us about prayer. Paul named three promises in this classic prayer passage:

> *Be anxious for nothing, but in everything by prayer and supplication, with thanksgiving, let your requests be made known to God; and the peace of God, which surpasses all understanding, will guard your hearts and minds through Christ Jesus (Phil. 4:6-7).*

The Promise Of God's Peace. The antidote to anxiety is prayer. The commitment of God is that when we roll our burdens onto His shoulders, He will give us peace. Many Christians will testify that in the dark night of fear when they brought their burden to the Lord, He gave them peace and they could sleep (Ps. 4:8). Therefore, we can rejoice to know that when we bring our concerns and burdens and cares to the Lord, He will give us peace.

The Promise Of God's Protection. Our minds and hearts will be protected when we pray. He who is our fortress guards us when the enemy attacks (Ps. 31:1-3). Therefore, we can rejoice in the protection we know He gives us.

The Promise Of God's Presence. Paul expressed it this way: "The God of peace will be with you" (Phil. 4:9). In our storm, going through the valley, or when we feel the most alone, prayer reminds us of God's presence. We can rejoice in His promise to be with us wherever we may be.

PRAYING THROUGH THE BIBLE

The Scriptures were written by people who felt the same desires and faced the same discouragements as we do. They too were dismayed at times by their circumstances. They knew what it was like to cry out to a silent God, to come to the end of themselves, and to feel their emotions going "over the edge." Yet the people of the Bible are important to us because they lived long enough to recover their sense of joy and confidence in God.

As we struggle through our own fears and disappointments, we can find renewed hope by using their thoughts as a reflection of our own hearts and prayers. Psalm 42 is a good example. With a thirsty, downcast soul, the author cried out to the Lord and expressed the honest emotions of his heart until he rediscovered truths he had forgotten.

First we will quote a verse, then we'll show how you might pray, based on what the verse says:

"As the deer pants for the water brooks, so pants my soul for You, O God. My soul thirsts for God, for the living God. When shall I come and appear before God?" (Ps. 42:1-2).

Lord, those words express how empty I feel. I feel so dry and tired and weak from running. My strength is gone. I don't know how much longer I can go on. If You don't help me I'm not going to make it.

I know that someday I will stand before You. But I long to hear from You now. What do You want from me? What do You want me to do?

"My tears have been my food day and night, while they continually say to me, 'Where is your God?'" (v.3).

Father, I do wonder where You are and why You aren't helping me. I've been so open in the past about trusting You. But now I feel uncomfortable when I'm with people who have heard me talk about how faithful and trustworthy You are.

"I went with them to the house of God, with the voice of joy and praise" (v.4).

Things used to be so different, Lord. I used to enjoy You in the presence of Your people. We laughed and prayed together. Yet now I feel so alone. Those times of joy seem so far away.

"Why are you cast down, O my soul? And why are you disquieted within me? Hope in God, for I shall yet praise Him" (v.5).

Yes, Father, I too know better. As I listen to my own complaint, I know deep inside that You can still be trusted. I do know that it is right to keep on trusting You. Like the psalmist, I even believe that in Your wisdom, and at the right time, You will help me. I know I will laugh again. I know the day is coming when I will praise You. O Lord, how I long for that day.

"The Lord will command His lovingkindness in the daytime, and in the night His song shall be with me—a prayer to the God of my life" (v.8).

I do believe that the day is coming when You will again let me experience Your kindness. I believe that You will once again give me songs in the night.

"I will say to God my Rock, 'Why have You forgotten me? Why do I go mourning?'" (v.9).

Father, even though I know You will help me, my fears keep coming back over me like waves. In spite of my faith in You, and even though I know You are my rock and my hiding place, I still feel so forgotten and alone. Why do You have to let me, Your child, spend my time mourning rather than praising You?

"Why are you cast down, O my soul? And why are you disquieted within me? Hope in God; for I shall yet praise Him, the help of my countenance and my God" (v.11).

Yes, I will yet praise You, Lord. You are my only hope. I praise You for Your goodness. Forgive me for doubting You. I will wait for You. I will wait for You to restore my joy!

BIBLE PASSAGES TO PRAY THROUGH WHEN:

- **In Danger:** Psalm 91
- **Depressed:** Psalm 34, 139
- **Worried:** Philippians 4
- **Facing A Crisis:** Psalm 121
- **Discouraged:** Psalm 23, 42; Isaiah 40
- **Tempted:** Psalm 1; 1 Corinthians 10
- **Lonely:** Psalm 27
- **Needing Courage:** Joshua 1
- **Seeking Forgiveness:** Psalm 32, 51
- **In Doubt:** Hebrews 11
- **Needing Assurance:** Romans 8; 1 John 5
- **Thankful:** Psalm 136
- **Joyful:** Psalm 100

YOUR NEXT PRAYER

Your next prayer could change your life. Go back to page 2. How did you fill in the blank? Are any of the disappointments on page 3 affecting you?

It's time to act. Ask God to help you make the decision to push through those roadblocks, overcome those hindrances, and begin praying as you'd like to. If you get discouraged, don't let that stop you. The Puritans had a saying, "Pray until you pray." Keep praying. You will soon pray with renewed confidence.

On the other hand, it could be that you need to start with the most basic step of all. Perhaps as you've read this booklet, you've sensed that you are not sure you have a personal relationship with God. You realize that you are a sinner (Rom. 3:23). But you also need to know this:

- You can't save yourself (Eph. 2:8-9).
- Jesus, the sinless Son of God, lived the perfect life we could never live (1 Pet. 2:22).
- Jesus died on the cross to pay the penalty for all our sin (1 Cor. 15:3-4).
- Christ's resurrection is proof that His sacrifice was acceptable to God (Rev. 1:4-6).
- We receive the Lord as our Savior by faith (Jn. 3:16).

Ask God to save you from the deserved penalty of your own sins. Trust Him to rescue you. You will find that this request will be the most important prayer you will ever pray. It is this prayer for salvation that provides an unshakable foundation for all of the other prayers you will offer up to God.